Percussion

intermediate level

MASTER SOLOS
by Peter Magadini

Edited by Linda Rutherford

The first three snare drum solos are unaccompanied solos. The percussionist should play along with a metronome or with the click track on the recording for extra practice.

HAL•LEONARD®
CORPORATION
7777 W. Bluemound Rd. P.O. Box 13819 Milwaukee, WI 53213

Visit Hal Leonard Online at
www.halleonard.com

Introducing

Mr. Peter Magadini

Mr. Magadini is a musical innovator and his credentials as a performer, scholar, author, and educator are outstanding. As a drummer and percussionist, he has played with many and diverse artists and organizations including the George Duke Trio, Diana Ross, Don Ellis Band, John Handy Quintet, Mose Allison Trio, the Berkshire Music Festival Orchestra, the Toronto Symphony Orchestra, the Hamilton Symphony Orchestra, and the Fromm Festival of Contemporary Music at Tanglewood. In addition, Mr. Magadini has performed as a studio musician in San Francisco, Los Angeles, and Toronto.

Mr. Magadini holds a Bachelor of Music from the San Francisco Conservatory of Music and a Master of Music from the University of Toronto. He has had teaching experience at the San Francisco Conservatory, Los Angeles Professional Drum Shop, the Lake Tahoe Concord Summer Music Camp, and has taught privately throughout his career. Mr. Magadini has studied with Donald Bothwell, Roy Burns, and timpani virtuoso Roland Kohloff, to whom he dedicates this book. As a clinician, he is known in the United States and Canada and was recently nominated to the Avedis Zildjian Hall of Fame.

This series of solos conforms to many of the requirements of the numerous Solo and Ensemble Contest Festivals. They have been chosen so that each piece will present to the adjudicator the elements of performance so necessary to a correct evaluation. The time limitation is also a consideration so the length of each has been structured in the two to four minute length.

More specifically, the material had the following objectives:

1. To present quality music in different rhythmic styles, such as classical, jazz, South American, and Afro-Cuban as applied to traditional and contemporary percussion techniques.
2. To keep the difficulty of the solos within the technical limits of this particular level.
3. To select solos which could improve your artistic and technical capabilities.
4. To present in each piece some examples of the principle categories of the grading, such as Technic, Rhythm, Articulation, and Interpretation.

Mr. Magadini will perform each solo on the tape. After each solo, you will hear a practice track. For the three unaccompanied snare drum solos, a metronome click has been provided for you. For the other solos, the accompaniment will be played. You can be the soloist on this track. It can also be a study guide for your accompanist.

It is our hope that you will enjoy this innovative approach to music study and development. The care in preparation is of course the prime factor in a successful presentation.

HAL•LEONARD®
CORPORATION
7777 W. BLUEMOUND RD. P.O. BOX 13819 MILWAUKEE, WI 53213

Rudimental Review

Many percussionists feel that there are really only two fundamental rudiments involved in snare drum technique, not the thirteen or twenty-six usually taught. These two rudiments are made up of combinations of single strokes and double strokes.

A. SINGLE STROKES

R L R L R L R L etc.

Single strokes are comprised of one tap for each hand and alternate from one hand to the other.

Using either the matched grip or the traditional grip (over-under grip) practice single strokes. You can begin with either the right or left hand. Let the stick strike the drum with a solid blow. This allows the stick to absorb the energy of the impact and rebound with the hands naturally. It is important to remember that a snare drum stick will give you the best results when you allow the stick to bounce on its own rather than trying to force the rebound with your hands.

Good technique is learning to control the natural bounce of the stick.

B. DOUBLE STROKES (BOUNCE STROKES)

R R L L R R L L R R L L R R L L etc.

When you are playing double strokes slowly, it is much like playing single strokes as you will control each tap. As you play faster, the second tap changes to a stick bounce. You will strike the drum once and the natural rebound of the drumstick makes the second tap automatically. You still must learn to control this tap. Think of controlling it like you would control a bouncing basketball.

1. The Open Roll

The open roll is a series of double bounces played at a fast predetermined speed. The important thing to remember about the open roll is that the drum sticks never play more than two taps in each hand, no matter how fast the roll is played.

Open rolls can be played in a variety of rhythms depending on the tempo of the music.

2. The Closed or Buzz Roll

The buzz roll, often referred to as the closed or press roll, is a series of buzz sounds from each alternating stick.

To begin developing your buzz roll, play a short relaxed buzz with each stick. Be careful not to tense your hands as you play.

After you can play a clear buzz in each hand, increase the speed until the "buzz" connects into one continuous sound.

There are several things that can affect the sound of the buzz roll:

a. The weight of the stick. It is suggested that you use a heavier stick when playing a buzz roll.

b. The tension and tuning of the drum head. The batter head should be fairly tight.

c. The adjustment of the snares. The snares should be adjusted so they respond sensitively to the soft buzz of the stick.

d. The size of the drum in terms of depth. The concert snare drums will respond better because they are not as deep as a parade drum.

e. The volume of the roll. A loud roll will produce a buzz of shorter duration so the strokes must be alternated faster to compensate. The softer the volume the less motion there is between the hands.

f. The style of the music. Buzz rolls are primarily used in symphonic music and in some concert band music. A very general rule you may want to follow is to play all rolls as closed (buzz) rolls unless the music or the conductor indicates otherwise.

Short Rolls

An easy way to memorize short rolls is to figure out how many hand movements are required. To do this, take the number of the roll (5-stroke) and divide it by 2. ($5 \div 2 = ②\frac{1}{2}$). Take that whole number (2) and add 1. (2 + 1) The 5-stroke roll has 3 basic hand movements.

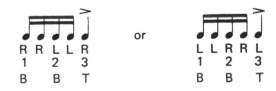

A 7-stroke roll would have four main hand movements.
$(7 \div 2 = ③ \frac{1}{2} + 1 = 4)$

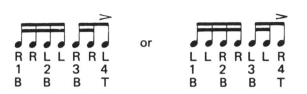

The same formula applies to the remaining rudimental
roll patterns:

9-stroke	$9 \div 2 = ④ \frac{1}{2} + ① = 5$
11-stroke	$11 \div 2 = ⑤ \frac{1}{2} + ① = 6$
13-stroke	$13 \div 2 = ⑥ \frac{1}{2} + ① = 7$
17-stroke	$17 \div 2 = ⑧ \frac{1}{2} + ① = 9$

C. GRACE NOTE RUDIMENTS

The grace note rudiments are made up of combinations
of single and double strokes.

1. The Flam

Remember that the grace note strikes the drum first
and the main note strikes the drum immediately
after the grace note. The hand playing the grace note will
always be closer to the drum head. When one flam
is played, the hands reverse so the hand that played
the main note now will play the grace note. Always
aim to keep the grace note hand still and close to
the drum when you are switching hands for the next
flam.

2. The Drag

The drag is much like the flam except it has two grace
notes preceeding the main note. These two grace notes
can be played "open" or "closed".

The open grace notes will have two distinct beats before
the main note.

Open grace notes are played mainly in concert band, marching band, or rudimental drumming.

The closed grace notes will have a short buzz before the main note.

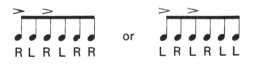

Closed grace notes are played primarily in orchestral music and sometimes in concert band music.

Throughout this book you should play the drags closed unless the music or your teacher specify otherwise.

3. Ruff (3-stroke and 4-stroke)

The 3-stroke ruff is like the drag except that the grace notes are played with alternate strokes rather than double strokes. The 4-stroke ruff has three grace notes preceeding the main note. Likewise these are played with alternating strokes.

D. COMBINATION RUDIMENTS

1. The Single Paradiddle

Probably the most well-known of the "combination" rudiments is the single paradiddle. It is the combination of two single strokes and a double stroke.

R L R R   or   L R L L

2. The Double Paradiddle

The double paradiddle is a combination of four single strokes and a double stroke.

R L R L R R   or   L R L R L L

3. The Triple Paradiddle

The third paradiddle is the triple paradiddle. It is a combination of six single strokes and a double stroke.

R L R L R L R R   or   L R L R L R L L

The Rhythm Piece

musical terms

moderato	in a moderate, easy-flowing tempo
sfz	sforzando, forced, giving a strong accent
al	to
Coda	a section added at the end of the music
D.S. al Coda	go back to the sign, play through the music to the coda sign, then skip to the coda section to finish the piece

In each of the solos in this book, you'll see marking like . . .

M.M. ♩=108. The M.M. stands for Maelzel's Metronome, the inventor of the metronome. This particular marking means that the metronome should be set at 108 and each click represents the length of a quarter note. These indications are suggestions of a tempo. If at first you cannot play the solo at this tempo, practice it slower and gradually increase the speed as you learn it. If this tempo is too fast for you to perform well, play it at a speed that is comfortable for you.

Measures 1-10 Be sure to count carefully throughout the solo. Be aware of the quarter note beat either by thinking of it or using a metronome.

You should alternate the strokes throughout the composition and work out the stickings that will <u>generally</u> set up your strongest hand for the beginning of each measure. You should also take into account the flow of the music. You'll notice in the following illustration that in measure 2 you do not change the sticking on the first beat but wait until the quarter rest on beat 3.

ILLUSTRATION 1

Practice the following exercise to develop your ability to play single strokes evenly and precisely. Begin the exercise slowly, get faster, then end it by slowing down. Be sure to rotate your hands with a maximum wrist turn in accordance with the natural rebound of the stick.

You'll notice that as the notes get faster, the rebounds are closer to the drum head. As the notes slow down the rebounds begin to move further away from the drum until you have arrived back at the original tempo and maximum wrist turn.

PREPARATION 1

In measure 4 you have a new rhythm called a triplet. This triplet divides a quarter note into three equal parts. Be sure to crescendo firmly from "mf" to "f".

In the next measure you have sixteenth notes used in various combinations. Practice the following exercises to become familiar with the different rhythm patterns used in this solo.

PREPARATION 2

PREPARATION 3

Measures 11-24 Be sure to count carefully during your measures of rest. One way to keep your place when you are counting is to say the measure number instead of one at the beginning of the measure. For instance:

ILLUSTRATION 2

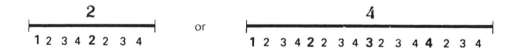

| 2 | | 4 |
| 1 2 3 4 **2** 2 3 4 | or | 1 2 3 4 **2** 2 3 4 **3** 2 3 4 **4** 2 3 4 |

Observe the accents beginning in measure 17 carefully. Be sure to play these notes louder.

Diminuendo evenly from "f" to "mf" throughout measure 22. Begin measure 23 softly and get gradually louder to the "sfz" in measure 24. The accents should be played in relation to the dynamic level. Accents in a piano (p) passage are softer than the accents in a mezzo forte (mf) passage.

Remember to repeat back to measure 3. When you play to the coda sign (To Coda ⊕) at measure 10, skip down to the Coda section beginning at measure 25. This passage is marked with the coda sign (⊕ CODA) and will end the piece.

The Rhythm Piece

Peter Magadini

The Dawn Drum

musical terms

largo	very slowly
field drum	a parade drum with snares — a deep sounding snare drum

"The Dawn Drum" is a solo piece in a very slow tempo. One of the first functions of the drum from the beginning of history was to make announcements. The drummers of ancient times played soldiers into battle, announced retreats, and played for executions and funerals.

"The Dawn Drum" is a piece that should be played as if for a sad occasion such as a last tribute. All rolls in the piece are closed (buzz) rolls and should be metered in sixteenth note triplets. Practice the following exercises to develop your technique of playing buzz rolls.

Start a buzz roll very softly. The hands should move just fast enough to connect the buzz of each alternating stick. The amount of stick pressure should be the weight of the

drum stick only.

Once you have attained an even, smooth soft roll, begin to apply pressure to the stick. Add the pressure by tightening the grip of the index finger and thumb of both hands in matched grip. (For the over-under grip tighten the index finger and thumb of the right hand and the thumb only of the left hand.) At the same time you are tightening your grip, you should press harder into the drum head.

When you add pressure to the roll, the duration of the buzz is shorter. To keep the roll connected and smooth you must increase the speed of the alternating hands. Practice this exercise for one or two minutes each day to develop a good clean buzz roll.

PREPARATION 4

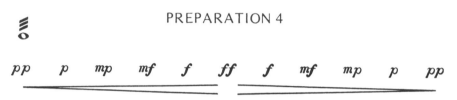

At this slow tempo the rolls will connect best when the hands are alternating in sixteenth note triplets. Practice the following exercise until you can play a smooth, even roll.

ILLUSTRATION 3

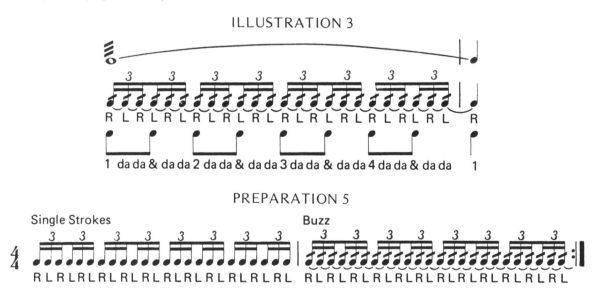

PREPARATION 5

Also, all drags are closed and the grace notes should be played close to the main note. Practice playing drags in closed style in the following exercise. Begin slowly, get gradually faster, and then grow slower to finish.

PREPARATION 6

Measures 1-8 Remember that the hands should move in sixteenth note triplets to keep the buzz roll smooth and even. You should alternate the flams in measure 2.

ILLUSTRATION 4

All of the drags and ruffs should alternate with the grace notes close to the main note. The drags should be played closed.

ILLUSTRATION 5

Closed Drag

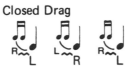

ILLUSTRATION 6

4-Stroke Ruff

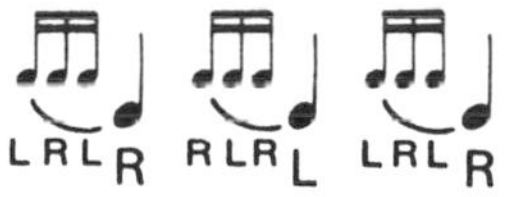

During the three beat rest in measure 8 move the snare release to off. Now the drum will sound like a tom-tom. Play the repeat of the first section without snares.

Measures 9-17 In measure 9 use the two beat rest to put the snares back on. Remember to alternate the drags throughout the solo.

In measure 16 the rolls should be played as closed 7-stroke rolls.

ILLUSTRATION 7

Play the triplets cleanly while crescendoing into measure 18.

Measures 18-25 The section is a repeat of the first section. Review the points discussed earlier.

To help you organize the solo in your mind think of the overall form. Measures 1-8 are section A, measures 9-17 are section B and measures 18-25 are a repeat of section A. The form of "The Dawn Drum" then is A A B A.

The Dawn Drum

Peter Magadini

A Sentimental March

musical terms

molto — more

D.C. al Coda — go back to the beginning, play through the music to the coda sign, then skip to the coda section to finish the piece.

This solo is an effective, interesting march. Practice the following preparation to review playing 6/8 time. Remember that you count a faster 6/8 time in two beats so the strong beats fall on beats 1 and 4 of the group of six.

PREPARATION 7

Metronome
Pulse

Measures 1-11 The rolls in this solo should be played closed and metered in sixteenth notes. Look at the illustration below which shows the roll in the first measure.

ILLUSTRATION 8

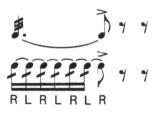

R L R L R L R

Practice the following exercises to develop a smooth closed roll. Be sure to move smoothly from one hand to the other as you play.

PREPARATION 8

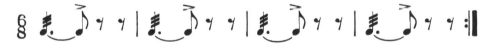

Whenever you are playing tied rolls, move into the single tap without pausing.

Watch the dynamics from "ff" to "mf" and alternate the sticking. Begin to crescendo back to "ff" in measure 6.

You have played flam taps before but now you will be playing them in 6/8 time. Be sure to play the tap with the stick that is kept close to the drum head.

ILLUSTRATION 9

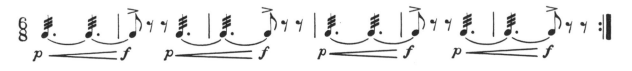

L R   R R L   L

Measures 12-22 Begin this section with a drop to a piano (p) dynamic level and crescendo into a forte (f). Practice crescendoing through two beats and be sure to play the accents. Remember, the roll should be played closed.

PREPARATION 9

p ⟨ f   p ⟨ f   p ⟨ f   p ⟨ f

Measures 23-54 In measure 23 several groups of shorter rolls (5-stroke rolls) are introduced. Be sure to play these rolls closed and with alternate sticking.

PREPARATION 10

R L L   R R   L L   R R   L L   R R   L L   R

The roll in measure 27 can be thought of as a closed 9-stroke roll in which the hands move with the five basic motions of a 9-stroke roll.

ILLUSTRATION 10

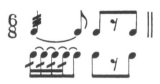

In measure 29 there is a new rudiment called the flam accent. Practice this alternating rudiment moving from a slow tempo to a fast tempo and back to a slow tempo.

PREPARATION 11

ᴸR L RᴿL R L   ᴸR L RᴿL R L   ᴸR L RᴿL R L   ᴸR L RᴿL R L

In measure 33 there is a series of 5-stroke rolls ending with an accent. Practice this measure several times to become familiar with the pattern.

PREPARATION 12

Go back to the beginning for the repeat. Remember that the first section is played two times before you skip down to the coda section to end the piece.

Measures 35-42 In measure 39 there is another series of 5-stroke rolls but in this measure the accent begins the measure instead of the roll. Practice this pattern several times to get the feel of the rhythm.

PREPARATION 13

Watch the dynamics carefully throughout and play the solo with authority and confidence.

A Sentimental March

Peter Magadini

Toronto Samba

musical terms

allegro	moderately fast
subito	suddenly
cadenza	a section with freer rhythms or that is to be improvised with the soloist's personal inflections. — This section usually comes at the end of a solo.

This piece is to be played on two tom-toms. Although no special pitches are required, the drums should be tuned with the interval of approximately a third between them. The tom-toms should be placed with the higher pitched drum on the performer's right. Always stand in front of the piano and close enough so both you and your accompanist can hear well.

The rhythmic theme in this solo is South American. There should be a relaxed feeling to the solo to help give the rhythms room to flow. Remember a samba is a dance and should be played in the style of a dance.

Practice measures 9-12 several times with your accompanist to get the feel of the music. Watch all of the dynamics carefully.

Measures 1-26 This first two measures of the solo set the pattern of the samba. This is the samba pattern that was taught to me by a percussionist from Argentina. Practice these measures several times slowly at first; then, gradually faster. Preferably you should practice with the metronome.

PREPARATION 14

Notice that the accents in the first measure are with the basic pulse through beat 3. When the right hand doubles the stroke on beat 3, the accent becomes syncopated or moves off of the beat. Again in the second measure the double strokes cause the accent to move, now on the beat.

This pattern is the rhythmic theme and should be memorized. It is fun to play and very interesting.

Along with the samba rhythm this solo concentrates on the technique of combining single and double strokes.

The most well-known combination is the single paradiddle. Practice this rudiment as you have other rudiments beginning slowly, getting gradually faster, and then slowing down again. Be sure to always count so that you will be playing the sixteenths evenly.

PREPARATION 15

Measures 1 through 15 have been made up of the samba beat, single strokes, or single and double paradiddles. Beginning in measure 16 you will begin playing single and double strokes in a random mixture. To help develop this skill, practice the following exercises. Be sure to practice as you did before. Begin slowly, gradually speed up, and then

slow down again. Always count carefully so you will be playing the sixteenths correctly.

In this exercise the pattern throughout is a right single stroke and left double strokes.

PREPARATION 16

Now switch the pattern to a left single stroke and right double strokes.

PREPARATION 17

Finally mix the single and double strokes. Remember to always begin practicing these exercises slowly, then gradually speeding them up.

PREPARATION 18

R L L R L L R R L L R L R L R R   L R R L R R L R L L R R L R R L

Measures 27-46 The samba rhythm returns in measure 27. This rhythm crescendos to measure 31 where it is condensed into one measure of sixteenth notes instead of eighth notes. Begin to diminuendo in measure 32.

Measure 33 moves into a different time signature — 3/4, and as a result the rhythmic flow of this section changes from eighth and sixteenth notes to triplets. To become familiar with changing time signatures practice the following exercise. Be sure to count aloud and keep the quarter note constant throughout.

PREPARATION 19

1 & 2 & 3 & 4 &   1 e & a 2 & a 3 e & a 4 e &   1 da da 2 & 3   1 e & a 2 & 3 da da

In measure 45 the 4/4 time signature returns to prepare for the repeat to the sign at measure 9.

Measure 9-14 Review the techniques of this section discussed earlier. When you arrive at the end of measure 14, be sure to skip down to the coda section beginning at measure 47.

Measures 47-55 The coda section of "Toronto Samba" is a cadenza. At one time in music history a cadenza was an improvised section that was usually found at the end of the solo. This would give the instrumentalist or vocalist an opportunity to display his or her virtuosity of improvisation and technique.

In later years a suggested cadenza began to be written in and most players relied on this written cadenza rather than improvising. In this solo, however, the cadenza is to be improvised.

To help you organize your improvisation keep two guidelines in mind:

1. The improvisation section must be eight measures long — measures 47 through 54, and it must be played in tempo.
2. The percussionist is to play only sixteenth note patterns.

The freedom of the solo evolves from the choice of drums, sticking patterns, dynamics, and accents.

Remember, this is an improvisation section so it should sound somewhat different each time you perform.

To prepare for the improvisation section practice the following exercise. You must remember that your improvisation must be done in the style and form set by the composer. Since this solo has emphasized the samba rhythm, you should keep that rhythm as a basic style.

PREPARATION 20

1. Play sixteenth notes in a steady tempo. Always count aloud.
2. On one drum, mix single strokes and double strokes and add accents.
3. After you feel comfortable doing this exercise on one drum, add the second tom-tom.
4. Again mix single strokes and double strokes on both drums and add accents.

The last measure is written out for you and must be played exactly as it is written. Concentrate on getting that first beat correct and the remainder of the measure will fall into place. The last three notes are to be played loudly and exactly with the piano.

Toronto Samba

Peter Magadini

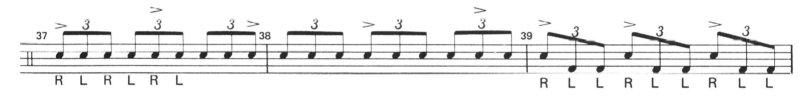

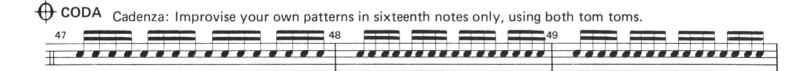

D.S. al Coda ⊕

⊕ **CODA** Cadenza: Improvise your own patterns in sixteenth notes only, using both tom toms.

Mallet Percussion

The mallet family of percussion instruments consists of four basic instruments, each with a chromatic keyboard similar to the piano. The bars of the instrument, the keyboard, are made of rosewood or metal and are played with a variety of mallets.

A. Orchestra Bells (Glockenspiel)

The smallest instrument of the mallet family is the orchestra bells or glockenspiel. It has metal bars and generally a range of two and a half octaves. They are usually carried in a portable case which also functions as the frame which supports the bars when being played. The orchestra bells sound two octaves higher than the written range.

The orchestra bells have a marching counterpart which is called bell lyra. This name comes from the shape of the marching stand which is like a Greek lyre.

The timbre or quality of the instrument is a high pitched, piercing tone and the instrument is often used for this tone color in the high range of melodic passages.

Both the orchestra bells and the bell lyra are played with metal tipped, very hard rubber, or plastic tipped mallets. Because of the metal bars and these hard sticks, they have more resonance than the instruments with wooden bars. For this reason rolls are rarely used on bells.

To dampen the sound (stop the sound) the player must touch the resonating notes with the fingers, hands, or sometimes even the arms.

The ensemble parts for orchestra bells may be marked in other ways:

    Glock (abbreviation for glockenspiel)

    Campanelli (Italian)

    Jeu de Timbres (French)

      or most frequently

    Bells

B. Vibraphone (Vibraharp; Vibes)

The vibraphone is a relatively new percussion instrument in relation to the others. It was invented in 1916 and first employed in dance bands in the twenties. Although vibraphone parts may be found in orchestral music of today, this instrument is more often found in jazz ensembles. It is one of the favorite tools of the jazz percussionists and the featured solo instrument in many different kinds of modern music.

The vibraphone, like the bells, has metal bars. The range is usually three octaves and the sounding pitch is the same as the written pitch.

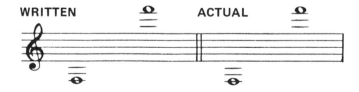

The mallets used on vibraphone vary from yarn or cord-covered sticks of various degrees of hardness to rubber, leather, or plastic tipped sticks and are used to achieve the different timbres possible on the instrument.

Generally the best known sound of the vibraphone is the mellow, velvet-like timbre and is accomplished by the use of the yarn mallets.

The vibraphone differs from the bells in two respects;

1) it has resonator tubes; and 2) it has a damper pedal. The resonator tubes amplify the sound. The damper pedal controls how long the sound resonates. When it is depressed, the notes are allowed to ring; and when it is released, the notes are dampened and will not resonate.

The vibraphone also has small metal discs in the resonating tubes which give the vibraphone a unique vibrato effect. This effect can be regulated from slow to fast by the variable speed motor which turns the discs.

C. Xylophone (Silifono, Italian; Xylophon, German)

The xylophone, the instrument we all learned as part of our alphabet (x is for xylophone), is one of the earliest known mallet percussion instruments. The name, xylophone, comes from the ancient Greek — xulon = wood; phone = voice. Although the instrument dates back to ancient times, it wasn't used in orchestral music until the 19th century (around 1800).

The xylophone has rosewood bars and resonating tubes under the bars. The range of the instrument (excluding the small portable xylophone) varies from two and a half to three and a half octaves.

Most music is written for the three or three and a half octave xylophone which is the most common instrument. The xylophone sounds one octave higher than the written range.

The three octave xylophone range is:

The sticks used on the xylophone vary from rubber or hard plastic to various degrees of yarn. The harder the mallet, the more percussive and penetrating the sound becomes. It is suggested that you play the exercises and solos in this book with a rubber-tip stick with rattan handles.

The timbre of the xylophone ranges from a rather piercing, percussive sound to a pleasing, soft percussive sound depending upon the mallets used.

The wooden bars of the xylophone make it imperative for the percussionist to develop a smooth single stroke roll. The wooden bars do not sustain a note so longer tones must be sustained by a smooth even roll.

D. Marimba

The largest instrument in the mallet percussion family is the marimba. Like the xylophone it has rosewood bars with large resonators. The range of the marimba is usually four octaves and the sounding pitch is the same as the written pitch.

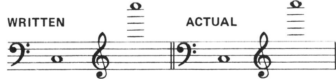

The marimba has a warm, deep sound and all of the techniques used for the xylophone may be applied to the marimba.

All of the solos and exercises in this book have been arranged with the xylophone in mind. However, they may be played on any of the mallet instruments.

There are two important aspects of mallet percussion playing that you should now begin developing. The first of these is striking the bars in the best place.

To get the cleanest sound and the best position for moving passages you should strike the lower keyboard in the center of the bar and the upper keyboard on the end near the lower keyboard. If the passage is slower, you can strike the upper keyboard in the center also. You should remember that the area around the cord is not a good place to strike because the sound is deadened and will not resonate properly.

The second technique you should begin to develop is sight reading. Because your hands do not actually touch the keyboard, you must develop a special sense of where the bars are. If you also watch the music and the conductor, you have added two additional skills to learn. There are some techniques that will help you begin developing these talents.

1. Move your music stand as close to the instrument as possible.
2. Lower the stand as close to the upper keyboard as possible.

By doing this your peripheral vision takes in some of the keyboard while you are reading the music.

You should also practice passages slowly, without looking at the keyboard too often.

Adagio

musical terms

adagio   slowly
dolce   sweetly, softly, prettily
legato   smoothly
accidentals   the notes of the upper keyboard which correspond to the black keys of a piano

This slow passage has been taken from Mozart's Serenade for Flute, No. 1 and has been transcribed (rewritten) for the xylophone. Since it is slow, it will give you an opportunity to develop the important technique of sustaining tones with a roll.

Remember that there are some areas of the bar which will resonate better than other areas. This is also true when you are playing rolls.

In addition the position of the hands will help you play better and faster. Hold the mallets with a matched grip,

relaxed position, with the thumb and index finger near the center of the mallet. The other fingers should be gently relaxed on the mallet handle.

Play the rolls with the left mallet positioned just in front of the right mallet at a 45° angle to the bar. For rolls on the lower keyboard you should play in the center of the bar. For the accidentals (notes on the upper keyboard) roll with the left hand in the center of the bar (behind the suspending string) and the right hand near the end of the bar (in front of the suspending string).

ILLUSTRATION 1

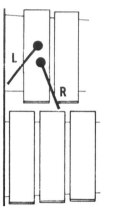

If a passage is fast you can play rolls on the upper keyboard with both mallets striking near the end of the bar (in front of the suspending strings). By playing rolls in this area there is less movement in the arms so you are able to move faster.

ILLUSTRATION 2

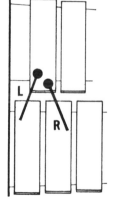

To begin developing your rolls, practice the following exercises. Keep the strokes even and relaxed at different speeds. Remember that these rolls are single alternating strokes, not double strokes.

PREPARATION 1

PREPARATION 2

PREPARATION 3

MASTER SOLOS
INTERMEDIATE
LEVEL

**Edited & Performed
by Peter Magadini**

Percussion

Solos for Snare Drum, Tympani, & Mallet Percussion

HAL•LEONARD®

Piano (Percussion)

intermediate level

MASTER SOLOS

by Peter Magadini

Edited by Linda Rutherford

The first three snare drum solos are unaccompanied solos. The percussionist should play along with a metronome or with the click track on the recording for extra practice.

HAL•LEONARD®
CORPORATION

7777 W. BLUEMOUND RD. P.O. BOX 13819 MILWAUKEE, WI 53213

Copyright © 1977 by HAL LEONARD CORPORATION
International Copyright Secured   All Rights Reserved

Toronto Samba

Peter Magadini

D.S. al Coda

CODA

Cadenza: Improvise your own patterns in sixteenth notes only, using both tom-toms.

R L R L R L R L L R
ff

f
ff

6

Adagio

Wolfgang Mozart
(1756-1791)

Trans. by P.M.

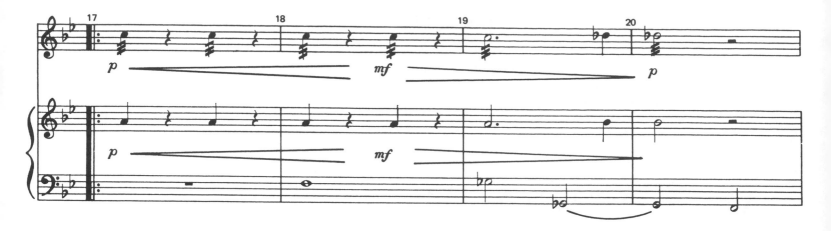

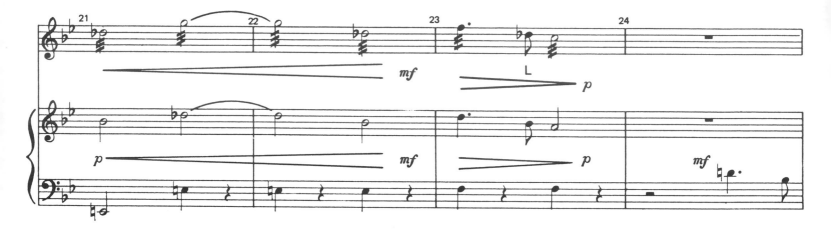

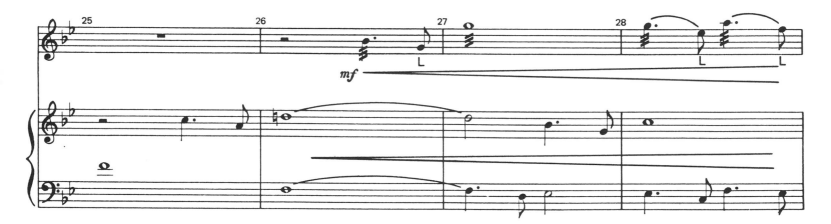

Allegretto

Franz Joseph Haydn
(1732-1809)

Trans. by P.M.

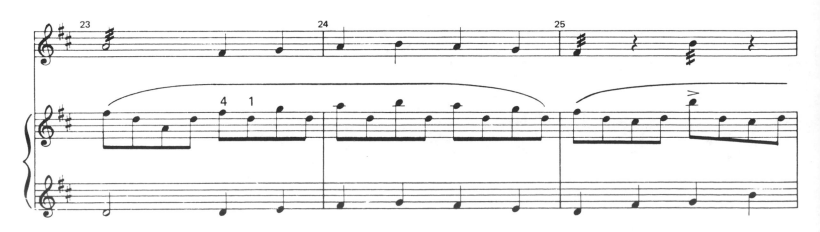

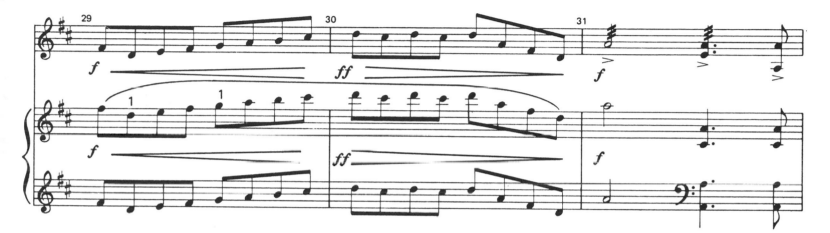

11

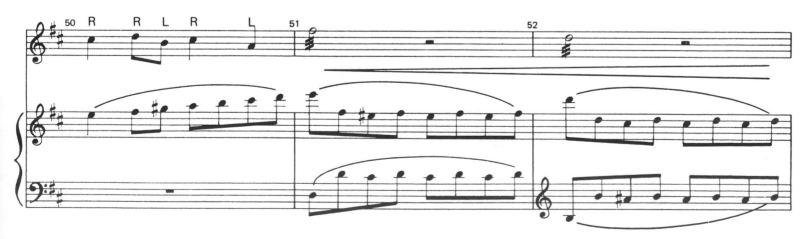

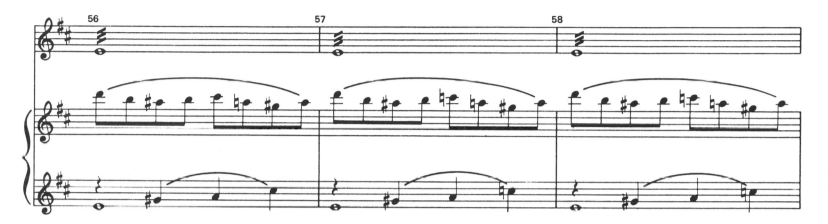

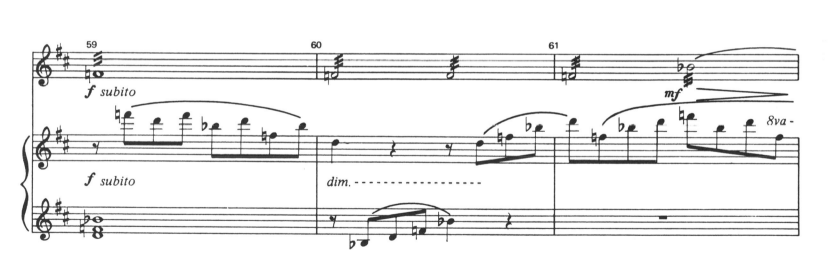

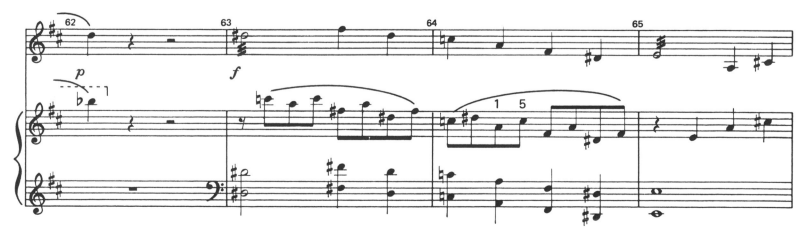

13

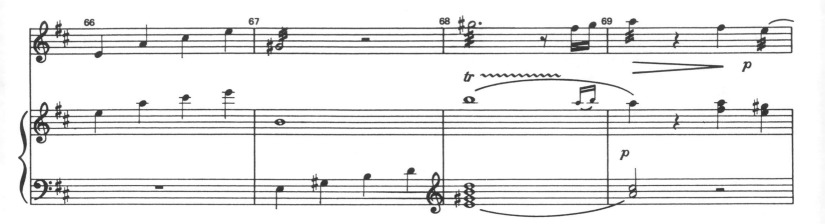

March

Johann Sebastian Bach
(1685-1750)

Tympani Part by P.M.

Stick To The Beat

Peter Magadini

(M.M. ♩ = 144)
Allegro
Jazz swing

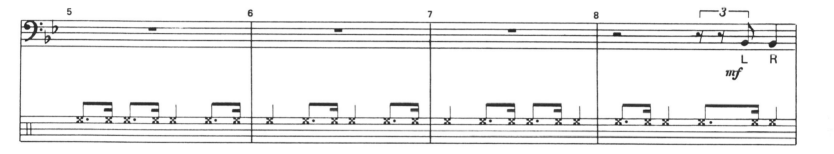

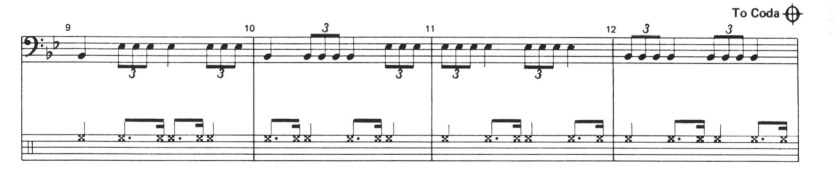

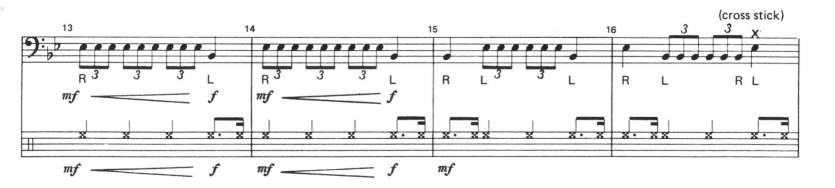

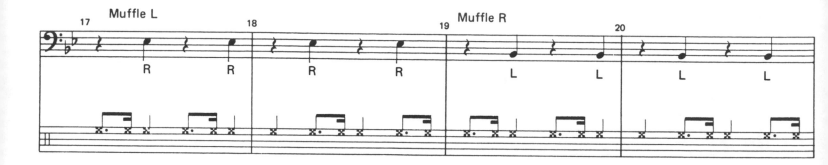

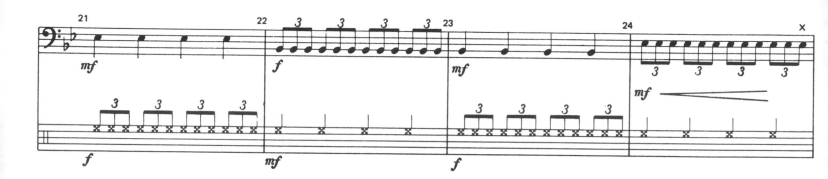

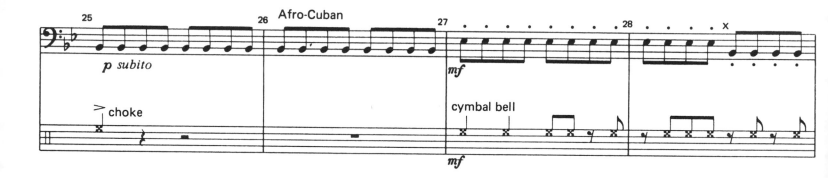

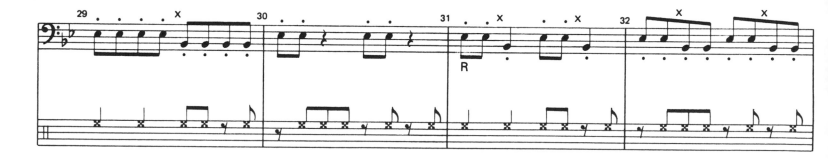

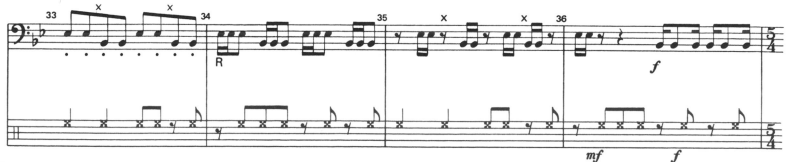

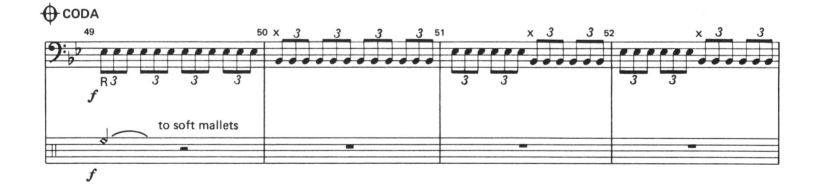

Now try this exercise which moves in skips rather than
by step.

PREPARATION 4

Practice quarter notes without rolls in this exercise.

PREPARATION 5

R L R L   R L R L   R L R L   R L R L   R L R L

Measures 1-7 This piece is to be played softly and
with an expression of beauty (dolce). Try to keep both
hands controlled with the same amount of pressure as you
play the rolls. Be sure to play the rolls for the full value
of the note. If you are playing a whole note, roll for
the full four counts. Always keep a count going in your
mind. The speed of the rolls is independent of the counting
but the counting will help you play the rolls for their
full value.

ILLUSTRATION 3

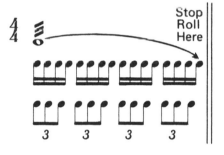

Be sure that you change from note to note evenly and do
not alter the character of the roll. The rolled "D" in
measure 3 should move directly into the struck "C",
which follows, without any pause.

Your rolls generally start in your strongest hand (for
most people the right). If you are moving to a struck note
from a roll, you would generally use the left hand when
descending and the right hand when ascending. The two
exercises below will give you an opportunity to practice
this technique.

PREPARATION 6

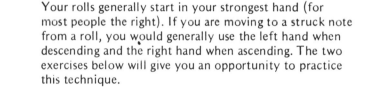

L   L   L   L   L   L   L

PREPARATION 7

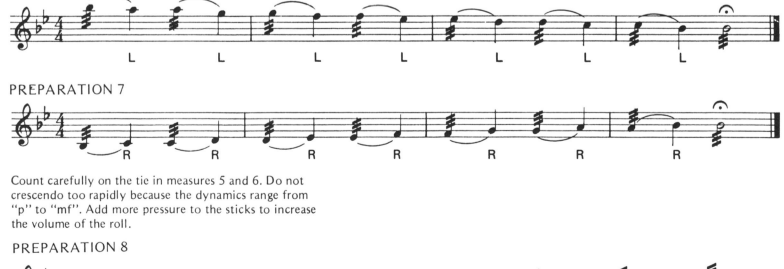

R   R   R   R   R   R   R

Count carefully on the tie in measures 5 and 6. Do not
crescendo too rapidly because the dynamics range from
"p" to "mf". Add more pressure to the sticks to increase
the volume of the roll.

PREPARATION 8

$p < mf > p$ $< mf > p$ $< mf > p$ $< mf > p$ $< mf > p$ $< mf > p$ $< mf > p$ $< mf > p$

Measures 8-16 In measures 9 through 12 connect smoothly and evenly. Don't forget to go back to the beginning for the repeat.

Measures 17-25 The quarter note rolls in measures 17 and 18 should last for only one full count. Be sure that you play them accurately so you will be with the piano.

Measures 26-33 The crescendo and decrescendo beginning in measure 26 lasts a longer length of time and it also moves to a higher dynamic level, "f", than in the previous phrase. Judge the rate of the crescendo and decrescendo carefully. In this music, dynamics should be played very subtly.

In measure 29 and 30 there is a passage of single notes. As a general rule single notes should be played with a minimum of stick crossing. In this particular passage the stickings have been indicated.

One thing to remember in single stroke playing is that you should be consistent. Practice the following exercise to begin developing your awareness of sticking patterns. Always begin to practice slowly and then gradually get faster.

PREPARATION 9

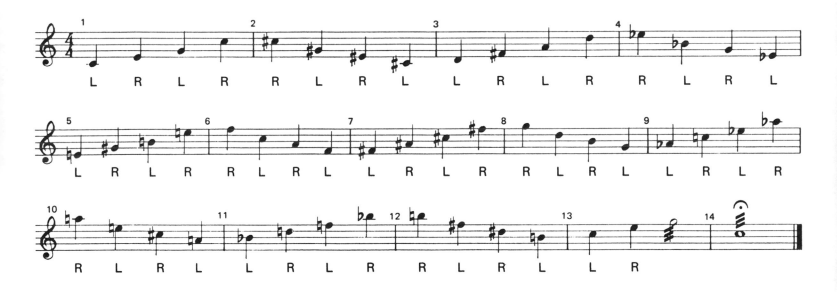

Be sure to practice with your accompanist several times to perfect this beautiful solo.

Adagio

Allegretto
musical terms

subito	quickly, immediately; generally used to indicate sudden changes in dynamics (subito p)
double stop	originally a term for strings meaning to play on two strings simultaneously. In percussion it means to play two notes simultaneously.

By using material written for other instruments such as oboe, flute, violin or voice or even transposing instruments such as trumpet or clarinet, the mallet percussionist has a wide choice of material. (Music for trumpet or clarinet is written in a different key than piano or xylophone so their part would have to be transposed.)

This solo has been taken from Haydn's Sonata No. 7 for violin. To adapt this solo for xylophone some notes have been changed to fit the mallet percussion technique.

Measures 1-8 Throughout this solo you will be playing double stops. This means that you will be playing two notes together. When these double stops are to be played as rolls, the right hand plays the top note and the left hand, the bottom note. The important thing is to make this roll as smooth and even as the roll you played on one note.

Practice the following chromatic exercise of double stops.

PREPARATION 10

The solo should start at a dynamic level of "f". When you come to measures 5 and 6 there should be a crescendo and decrescendo on the three rolls. Apply a bit of pressure to bring the dynamic level to "ff".

Measures 9-16 Begin the next section at a lower dynamic level, "p". Be sure to play the rolls evenly and to make the connection between the rolled notes and notes following very smooth. In measures 13 and 14 the rolls should be played at an even "p" dynamic level.

Measures 17-32 In measure 17 the character of the solo changes slightly with the introduction of the eighth notes. These should be played with a clean, even down-up technique. When you bring the mallets off the bar with this clean, upward wrist motion, you get the purest sound from the bar.

The following exercise will help you begin developing the clean down-up wrist action.

PREPARATION 11

Play the rolled quarter notes in measures 25-28 for their full value.

In measure 29 the stepwise eighth-note pattern returns followed by wider intervals. Practice the following exercise slowly and evenly to become familiar with this kind of pattern.

PREPARATION 12

Practice measure 31 slowly so you will be sure of the changes in the intervals. It may help to memorize this measure so you won't have to keep looking at the music.

Measures 33-62 For a contrast from the loud, moving passage begin this section softly. In measures 46-51 there are some special sticking patterns. Practice the following exercise several times to become familiar with these patterns. Be sure to start slowly and gradually move up to the speed of the solo.

PREPARATION 13

In measures 55 and 59 be prepared for the sudden changes in dynamics. One way you can do this is to train yourself to look ahead of the measure you are playing. These sudden changes of dynamics will add a flavor of surprise to the solo to make it more interesting.

Measures 63-80 The two sixteenth notes in measure 68 are a pick-up to the first note of measure 69.

PREPARATION 14

Beginning in measure 69 put a slight accent on the beginning of each rolled note that is tied.

ILLUSTRATION 4

Make the crescendo starting in measure 77 long and even building to a strong close. Be sure to keep the tempo steady and exact.

Allegretto

Franz Joseph Haydn
(1732 - 1809)

Trans. by P.M.

The Kettledrums-Tympani

(French: Timbales: Italian: Timpani, Timpano; German: Pauken)

The kettle drums first appeared in orchestral music around the late 1600's. From that time until the late 1700's most composers wrote for two kettledrums. These two drums were tuned to the tonic (first note) and dominant (fifth note) of the key signature. Beethoven first introduced a radical change in tuning in the early 1800's. In the later periods of music a third kettledrum was added and later a fourth.

The early kettledrums had animal hide heads and were tuned by turning hand tuning screws placed symmetrically around the head. As the tympani developed, calfskin was used exclusively for the heads and the foot pedal was introduced for tuning.

Today most tympani have plastic heads which are less affected by weather conditions. There are still some professional tympanists who prefer calfskin heads for clarity of tone.

Through the years several types of tuning mechanisms have developed. Today's tympani generally have two types. The machine drum is tuned by turning one large T screw that is connected to a chain around the drum. When the T screw is turned, the chain moves tuning sprockets to either tighten or loosen the head.

The other common type found today is the foot pedal. In this tympani the pitch is changed when the foot pedal is depressed or released. The following illustration shows one model available today.

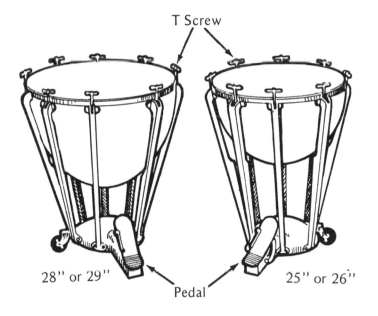

T Screw

28" or 29"   Pedal   25" or 26"

The two basic tympani sizes are 28" or 29" and the 25" or 26". The range for the 28" tympani is:

The range for the 25" tympani is: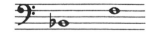

Place the tympani so that the 28" drum is on your left and the 25" drum is on your right. Arrange them so the tuning pedals are in an accessible spot. Also arrange them so you can strike each drum without hitting the T handles. A kettledrum is struck approximately 3 inches from the edge, never in the middle.

Before you begin playing, you should check the tuning of the heads. Choose a moderately low pitch on each drum by adjusting the pedal to a low point. Take a mallet and lightly strike the head close to the T handles (screws) around the drum. Listen to the pitch at each T handle carefully. All pitches should sound the same. If one sounds higher, the T handle is too tight. If one sounds lower, the T handle is too loose. When you have tuned each T handle, you have tuned the tympani with itself.

Next, check to see that the pedal operates up and down smoothly within the tuning range of each drum. You now can tune the tympani to the specific pitches of the music you are playing.

STICKS

There are basically four types of sticks that are used for tympani playing:

1. The general purpose stick made of a wooden ball wound with felt.

2. A softer cartwheel type stick that is used for quiet passages and soft rolls.

3. A harder stick made of a wooden ball with a very light covering that is used for staccato passages and rhythmic articulation.

4. An all wood stick that is used for loud, rhythmic articulation and for special effects.

The serious percussionist will probably own all of these sticks. Since the cost of professional sticks is high ($10 to $15 per pair), you may want to start with one pair of the general purpose variety. If you were to choose two pair, the next type you would probably want would be the lightly covered "staccato" stick.

GRIP

A good grip is essential. Turn your right hand palm up and place the stick across the first joint of the index finger. Place the thumb exactly across from the index finger and apply pressure. Gently rest the second and third fingers against the stick. The little finger does not contact the stick. Place the stick in the left hand in the same way.

Now turn your hands palm down and rest the sticks on the drum head. The sticks should form a V on the head and your elbows should be slightly away from your body.

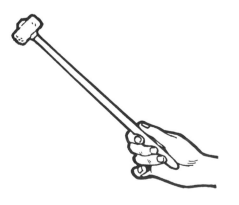

March

musical terms

allegro   lively

fp   a loud attack followed immediately by a soft dynamic level (p)

This march by Johann Sebastian Bach comes from a collection of piano pieces, <u>Notebook of Anna Magdalena Bach,</u> written for his daughter. This tympani solo was added to the piano solo especially for this book.

First, tune your tympani. Release the pedal so the drum is at its lowest pitch. Play a low "A" on the piano and hum the pitch to yourself. Now strike the drums and push down on the pedal. The note will slide up to the "A". If you go above the pitch, be sure to let the pedal out to the lowest pitch again and come up to the "A". It will be more precise and accurate if you move up to the pitch rather than move down.

Now have someone play the "A" on piano again, strike the drum, and check yourself.

Repeat the same process on the smaller drum with the pitch "D"

For extra practice tune the tympani to the pitches shown in the following exercise.

PREPARATION 1

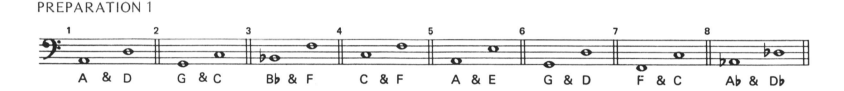

Remember that the lower notes are on the larger drum (28") and the higher notes are on the smaller drum (25").

Practice tuning every day to develop your ability.

Measures 1-9   Use the general purpose sticks. When playing single strokes on tympani, think of lifting the stick away from the head. This will bring out the full tone of the drum. Practice the following exercise to get the feel of this technique.

PREPARATION 2

All rolls on the tympani are moderately fast to fast single stroke rolls. The difference between rolls on xylophone and tympani is the speed. The tympani roll changes speed according to the volume and pitch.

Remember the following general rules:

1. The softer the dynamic level <u>or</u> the lower a pitch, the slower the roll should be played. This also means that the sticks are kept closer to the drum head.

2. The louder the dynamic level <u>or</u> the higher the pitch, the faster the roll should be played. This means that the sticks will be moving further away from the drum head.

In these exercises you will practice the roll at various dynamic levels and on different pitches. Remember that these variables will alter the speed of the roll and the **height** of the sticks above the drum head. Play each exercise several times and count carefully.

PREPARATION 3

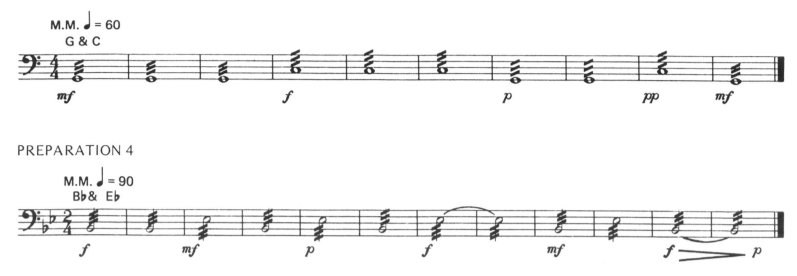

PREPARATION 4

On some notes you will want to stop the note on a drum so it will not ring through a rest or ring through a note played on the other drum. This technique is called muffling. For example, in measure 3 you need to stop the "D" from sustaining into the "A".

To muffle a ringing note, you must touch the drum head with the last three fingers in the exact spot where the head has been struck.

If the note to be muffled is followed by a rest, use the opposite hand to stop the ringing. If the note to be muffled is followed by another note, use the same hand to stop the sound at exactly the same time that you strike the next note. In measure 3 strike the "D" and let it ring for its full value. At exactly the same time you strike the "A" (with the left hand), muffle the "D" with the last three fingers of the right hand.

Practice the following exercise to become familiar with muffling the tympani.

PREPARATION 5

Remember to also muffle the "A" in measure 3.

In measure 4 you would not muffle the "D" since it is moving to a roll which requires both mallets.

Be sure to roll into the "D" when you go back to measure 1

for the repeat. Make the connection between these two measures smooth.

Measures 10-25 In measure 12 both the "A" and the "D" should be muffled on the fourth beat of the measure. The following exercise will give you practice in muffling both drums at the same time.

PREPARATION 6

When repeating the same note in a slow passage, it is not necessary to alternate sticking. It is actually preferable to play the notes with the same hand.

In measures 14 and 15 muffle the first note of each measure with the opposite hand. Practice the following exercise which incorporates muffling with the opposite hand.

PREPARATION 7

In measure 18 muffle only the "D" on beat three. The rolled "A" in measure 17 will have had sufficient time to decay.

When you are using general purpose tympani sticks and

you must play staccato notes, you should squeeze the shaft of the stick with the thumb and index finger, strike the drum firmly, and bring the sticks off the head immediately. Practice playing staccato notes in the following exercise.

PREPARATION 8

Muffle the "D" in measure 22 before you go back for the repeat. The tympanist will decide when a note should or should not be muffled. It is a technique that should be used only when there is time.

The last roll of the solo in measure 23 is marked with a "fp". Strike the drum with a solid blow. Let the volume diminish naturally to a soft dynamic level, then begin the roll and crescendo to a forte (f).

This solo has introduced several techniques that are essential for good tympani playing. Always listen carefully for proper dynamic levels and good musical interpretation.

March

Johann Sebastian Bach
(1685-1750)

Tympani Part by P.M.

Stick To The Beat

musical terms

jazz swing	style of music with a dance band feel
adagio	slow
a tempo	return to the original tempo

This solo provides the tympanist with an introduction to three rhythmic styles; jazz swing, Afro-Cuban, and a 5/4 adagio. To make it more interesting the accompaniment is provided by a ride cymbal rather than a piano. You should strive to make the transition into each style as smooth and connected as possible.

Tune carefully before you begin. Rehearse each section with and without the cymbal.

With the exception of the triplets in measures 21 and 23 and the roll in measures 55 and 56, the cymbal player should play all the cymbal parts with one hand. Keep

one pair of drumsticks and one pair of mallets within reach. The final cymbal note should be played with the handle of the mallet.

Measures 1-24 · You should use the general purpose tympani sticks for this solo. The first section is in jazz swing style. A dotted eighth-sixteenth is played as if it were the first and third notes of a triplet. This is the rhythm that the cymbal will be playing. The tympanist will be playing triplets so the two parts should fit together. Look at the following illustration which shows measures 8-10.

ILLUSTRATION 1

Count carefully so you enter at the correct time. Remember to count a series of rests like ①2 3 4②2 3 4③2 3 4④2 3 4, etc. This will help you keep track of the measures rest.

Your entrance in measure 8 comes on the third part of beat 3. Be sure to count carefully so you enter exactly.

ILLUSTRATION 2

Play even triplets with alternating strokes. The last beat in measure 12 should be in the right hand. The first beat in measure 13 should also be played with the right hand.

When playing tympani, you must learn to play the same dynamic level on both drums. To do this you will need to strike the lower pitched drum slightly harder to make the dynamic levels match. Practice the following exercise and strive to make the lower pitch as loud as the higher pitch.

PREPARATION 9

When moving from the third beat triplet to the fourth
beat quarter note in measure 16, you must cross the
left stick over the right. The stick that crosses over, either
the left or the right, must strike the exact beating spot of
the drum. Practice the following exercises to become familiar
with this technique. An X above the staff indicates where the
crossover occurs.

In measures 17-20 be sure to muffle the quarter notes with the opposite hand. The last note of measure 20 should be muffled with the left hand (same hand) at the same time you play the first note of measure 21 with the right hand.

Crescendo the triplets in measure 24 to a dynamic level of "f" and play the first note of measure 24 "subito p".

Measures 25-36 This begins the Afro-Cuban section of the solo. The cymbal rhythm changes to equal eighth notes and the part should be played on the bell of the cymbal. (The bell is the raised portion of the cymbal.)

The eighths and sixteenths played by the tympanist will fit with the rhythm of the cymbal. Carefully observe the staccato notes indicated throughout this section.

Be sure to start measure 34 with the right hand. This will eliminate the need for any cross sticking.

In measure 35 you must use cross sticking. Practice this measure slowly and accurately. Gradually increase the speed as you learn the pattern.

ILLUSTRATION 3

Both you and the cymbal player must be extremely precise in measure 36. The rhythms fit together as shown below.

ILLUSTRATION 4

Measures 37-48 The adagio section begins in this measure. Remember that adagio means slowly.

Above measure 37 you will see the indication ($\left. \right. = \left. \right.$). This tells you that a quarter in the adagio section is equal to a half note in the Afro-Cuban section. An easy way to play this is to have the beat of the Afro-Cuban section going in your mind. To get the tempo set at the beginning of measure 37, give each quarter note two beats at the tempo of the Afro-Cuban section,

count to yourself 1 & 2 & 3 & 4 & 5 &.

The 5/4 time signature may be new to you. There are five quarter beats in a measure.

Play the repeated "Eb's" with the right hand and the repeated "Bb's" with the left hand. This will help keep the dynamics and tempo even.

In measures 42 and 43 muffle the eighth note the same time you play the quarter note which follows. To become familiar with this pattern, practice the following exercise.

PREPARATION 18

Muffle all of the eighth notes in measure 44 with the opposite hand. In measure 44 begin to slow down to prepare for the "a tempo" in measure 48.

In measure 48 muffle both drums on the quarter rest of beat 3.

The last four eighth notes in measure 48 set up the tempo for the return to the beginning. (D.C. al Coda). One eighth note of the adagio section will equal one quarter note in the swing section at measure 1.

Play from measures 1-12 and skip to the coda section at measure 49.

Measures 49-54 Play the triplets "f" and exactly even. Watch for the cross sticking which occurs in this section.

In measure 55 start the roll with a "fp". Remember you strike the drum at a dynamic level of "f" and let the sound diminish naturally to the "p" you want. At that point you begin the roll. In these two measures crescendo the roll from the "p" to the "ff". Strike the "Eb" in measure 57 "ff" and immediately muffle both drums. If possible both drums should be muffled after a loud passage played on only one drum. The unplayed drum will still rumble from sympathetic vibrations. The cymbal note ends the solo so you must be able to hear it clearly.

Stick To The Beat

Peter Magadini

Adagio ($\half = \quarter$)

pp subito

Slightly slower

D.C. al Coda ($\eighth = \quarter$)

p — *mf* *a tempo* — *f*

⊕ CODA

f R

fp — *mf* — *ff*

41

Accessories

In addition to the major instruments — snare drum, tympani, and keyboard percussion — there a number of instruments that are important to the percussion player.

I. CYMBALS

One of the accessories to the percussion section are cymbals. Cymbals are probably the most individual instrument in the family and come in a variety of sizes, weights, and sounds. Cymbals are considered a pitchless instrument but a quality pair of cymbals should sound all of the notes and harmonic equivalents of the scale.

DANCE CYMBALS

Bop Cymbals (Be-Bop): A type of bounce cymbal, usually eighteen through twenty-four inches in diameter. They are especially tapered from cup out to produce the graduated range of pingy cymbal tones associated with modern jazz drumming.

Bounce Cymbals: (Also called "ride" or "top" cymbals): Usually eighteen through twenty-five inches in diameter. Bounce cymbals are designed to carry a sustained beat.

Crash Cymbals: Usually fourteen through eighteen inches in diameter: Normally crash cymbals are thin, medium-thin, or paper-thin in weight. They are struck for one or two cymbal beats at a time.

Crash-Ride Cymbals: These are medium, medium-thin, or thin cymbals, usually sixteen through twenty inches in diameter. They have the unique quality of being suitable for both crash work as well as for sustained ride cymbal playing.

Flanged Hi-Hats: (Also see Hi-Hats): Especially designed cymbals normally used as bottom cymbals of hi-hat pairs. They have flanged edges that increase the contact surface when top and bottom cymbals meet.

Hi-Hat Cymbals: (Also called "Sock cymbals", "Hi-boys", "Hi-socks", and "Off-beat cymbals".): Always a pair of two cymbals twelve through sixteen inches in diameter. They are mounted one above the other on a special stand controlled by a foot pedal. Hi-hats are matched on a basis of the blend of tone they make together — not necessarily by exact diameters or weights. There are hundreds of suitable combinations ranging from a larger cymbal over a smaller one all the way down to a thin hi-hat cymbal over a heavy band cymbal.

Ping Cymbals: Usually eighteen through twenty-four inches in diameter and medium to medium-heavy in thickness. A ping cymbal is designed to control the cymbal overtones so that they do not overpower the stick sound.

Ride Cymbals: See Bounce Cymbals.

Show Cymbals: These are crash-ride cymbals used to accent the kick beat for chorus lines, etc.

Sizzle Cymbals: Regular cymbals, eighteen to twenty-two inches in diameter, in which holes are drilled and rivets installed to give a sizzling or buzzing type of cymbal sound.

Although the size, weight, and fundamental tone (high, medium, or low) are important when choosing cymbals, the primary consideration is the type of music that is going to be played. The following glossary is reprinted by permission of Avedis Zildjian Company:

Splash Cymbals: (Also called Choke Cymbals): Small cymbals seven to eleven inches in diameter. They are usually thin in weight and are used for fast cymbal crash work and are very often choked off fast.

Swish Cymbals: Usually eighteen through twenty-two inches and shaped as illustrated ⎯⎯▲⎯⎯ Swish cymbals normally have rivets installed to give a Chinese tonal effect and are especially useful for playing Dixieland arrangements.

Top Cymbals: See Bounce Cymbals.

BAND AND ORCHESTRA CYMBALS

Band Cymbals: Paired cymbals, usually fourteen through sixteen inches in diameter, equipped with straps and pads (recommended) or handles. To fill the requirements of various types of marching bands these cymbals are available in medium-thin for band, medium for band and medium-heavy for band weights.

Concert Band Cymbals: Same as Symphonic Hand Cymbals except slightly heavier.

Crotales (Antique Cymbals): Small, thick cymbals sold in pairs ranging from two to five inches in diameter. They have very definite pitch and produce clear, unblemished notes when the edges are struck together. They are used to interpret special sounds in various classical works.

Drum Corps Cymbals: Similar to band cymbals except that they are heavier in weight, normally heavy and extra-heavy. This additional weight produces the more precise martial tone required in drum corps work.

Finger Cymbals: These are small, untuned cymbals usually about two inches in diameter. They are played together in various rhythms by dancers or by drummers playing for them.

Gongs (Tam-Tams): Large disk-shaped percussion instruments with no cups usually twenty-four through twenty-eight inches in diameter. They are available in thin (crashy), medium, and heavy (deep and mellow) weights. Gongs are suspended in rings mounted on heavy floor stands and are struck with a heavy (2-4 lbs.) padded mallet.

Hand Cymbals: An all-inclusive term used in describing any pair of cymbals equipped with straps and pads and played by striking together (i.e. Band cymbals).

Metal Castanets: A type of finger cymbal attached to steel spring handles and played by clicking together. They are normally used in Spanish or Oriental dance music.

Suspended Cymbals: Regular cymbals suspended on floor stands and played by striking with stick or mallet. They are usually fifteen through twenty-two inches in diameter. They range in weight from extra-thin through heavy depending upon the composition and the conductor's interpretation thereof.

Symphonic Hand Cymbals: These paired cymbals are usually seventeen through twenty-two inches in diameter. They are equipped with straps or straps and pads (never wooden handles) and are thin, medium-thin, medium, medium-heavy, and heavy in weight. They have a greater variety of tonal color than marching band cymbals. They fall into three general categories. 1. Germanic (or Wagnerian), heavy with a K-lang attack. 2. Viennese, medium-heavy with a Zzzing attack. 3. French, medium-thin to thin with a Ssswish attack.

CYMBAL TERMS

Bell Tone (Clear Tone): The fundamental (dominating) tone of a cymbal (without the overtones).

Chick, Chop or Chup Tone: The sound of hi-hats when they are played with the foot pedal only, the cymbals remaining together momentarily.

Ching Tone: The sound of hi-hats when foot is pressed lightly and released immediately allowing cymbals to meet and instantly separate.

Cymbal Bow: The gradually curving section from cup to edge of cymbal. (See Diagram)

Cymbal Cup (Bell): The center part of the cymbal which rises above the bow. (See diagram) Sometimes called the bell.

Flash Cymbal Tone: A fiery, crash tone found in a cymbal that has overtones only.

Marriage: The tonal blend which is used in pairing cymbals. Since quality cymbals produce many notes simultaneously rather than any of definite pitch, it is impossible to match them in sequence such as a fifth, third, etc.

Pinpointing the Beat: This is the function of band cymbals when played together with a bass drum. By pinpointing the beat of the drum the cymbalist emphasizes the rhythm and makes it crisper and more precise.

Response: The speed with which a cymbal answers after it has been struck (i.e. a fast cymbal is one that responds very quickly).

Roar or Spread: The overtones of a cymbal that sound when cymbal is rolled upon.

Weights of Cymbals: Inasmuch as there is a distinct difference in the weights used for dance work compared to those used for band and symphony work, it must be pointed out that all cymbals must be classified according to category before their weight can be classified (i.e. certain heavy dance cymbals can be the equivalent of a medium band or symphony cymbal in actual weight and at the same time completely different in playing characteristics. Medium-heavy for band is entirely different than medium-heavy for dance).

NOTE: The terms of this glossary are fundamental. The technical and slang expressions commonly used by drummers can usually be translated into one of the above terms.

A. Hand Cymbals

Grasp the leather straps with the thumb and index finger, then close the remaining fingers around the straps. Lift the cymbals chest high and hold them in a vertical position.

The cymbals should be struck with a glancing blow, not directly together. Hold the cymbals slightly apart. Now lower the right hand, and raise the left hand. To strike the cymbals start your right hand upward while the left hand starts downward quickly. The upper edge of the right cymbal makes the initial contact with the left cymbal just below the top edge. Complete the motion so that the entire surface of both cymbals make contact almost immediately. Let both hands keep moving to finish the cymbal crash. The right hand continues going up and the left hand down.

To stop the sound after the cymbal crash, bring the cymbals back to this vertical position and immediately draw them to your chest.

Practice playing crash cymbals in the following exercises. Be sure to observe all dynamic markings and to muffle the sound on the rests.

Example 1

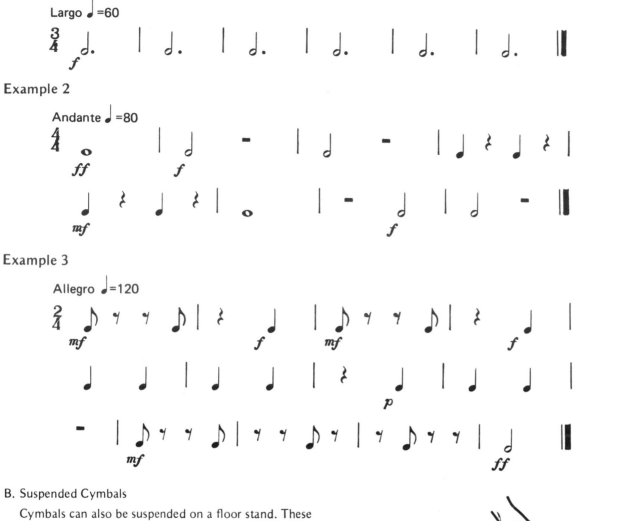

Example 2

Example 3

B. Suspended Cymbals

Cymbals can also be suspended on a floor stand. These are played with a variety of mallets or the snare drum sticks.

To muffle the sound the player grasps the outer edge of the cymbal with the free hand. If both hands are playing, then use either hand to muffle the sound.

Practice playing suspended cymbals in the following examples:

Example 1

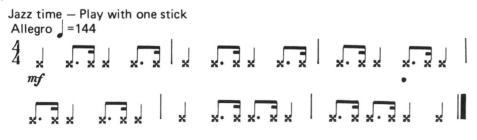

Example 2

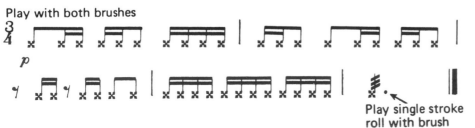

Play single stroke roll with brush

C. The Bass Drum (Italian, gran cassa; German, grusse trommel; French, grosse caisse)

The bass drum is the largest of the unpitched drums and should be struck off-center to produce the best sound.

The bass drummer should have a variety of sticks; one general purpose stick, one harder stick, and one pair of mallets for rolling. The general purpose stick will be used for most parts and the harder stick for staccato parts.

The roll on the bass drum is a single stroke roll. Most of the bass drum stands are adjustable so the player can tilt the drum at an angle to play the roll more comfort-ably. (It will also help if the sticks are held with the over-under snare drum grip in the left hand. The sticks will then clear the rim of the bass drum.)

The bass drum should be struck with a direct blow. The wrist should snap the stick away from the head immediately so the head can vibrate.

The head should be muffled on rests with the free hand. When both hands are being used, the drum can be muffled by touching the knee to the head.

Practice the following examples to perfect these bass drum techniques.

Example 1

Example 2

Example 3

D. Tambourine (Italian, tambaro basco; German, tambourin or or shellen trommel; French, tambour de basque)

The tambourine is a wood or metal frame with small metal discs called jingles attached. These jingles respond when the tambourine is struck or shaken. The sizes vary but the most common are 8", 10", and 12" diameter.

To play, hold the tambourine in one hand with the head face up. With the other hand strike the tambourine with the palm of the hand. Now clench the fist and practice striking the tambourine with the knuckles. Either of these two techniques can be used for most mezzo forte (mf) and forte (f) playing.

In the following exercises practice both techniques.

Example 1

Example 2

For soft passages the tambourine should be played with the tips of four fingers. Your thumb will rest against the index finger. Practice the exercises above with a dynamic marking of piano (p).

When you are playing extreme dynamic levels, there are special techniques that should be used. For very soft passages rest the tambourine head down on a cloth or towel-covered table. With <u>both</u> index fingers, play on the exposed rim in alternating strokes. Practice the following exercise in this manner.

Example 3

For fast, loud passages try the following technique. Hold the tambourine in one hand and strike the head (face down) against the knee. As the tambourine returns from striking the knee, strike the inside of the head with the knuckles of the free hand. To use this tech-

nique you may have to sit or raise the knee by resting your foot on a chair.

Start slowly and gradually increase the speed to develop this alternating method.

Example 4

Now practice alternating between the two strokes.

Example 5

Finally, a roll can be played on tambourine. The easiest and best way to play a roll is to hold the instrument perpendicular to the body and shake it back and forth slightly with a rapid motion. If the roll is tied, strike the instrument with the free hand (palm or fist) at the end of the roll.

Example 6

Roll Exercise
Allegro ♩=132

E. Triangle (Italian, triangolo; German, triangel)

The last accessory discussed in this book is the triangle. Like the cymbal, a good quality triangle will not sound a single note but a range of pitches and harmonies.

Hold the triangle with the clip so your fingers do not touch the triangle itself. Strike the base of the triangle with a metal beater and immediately lift it.

Practice the following exercise on the triangle:

Example 1

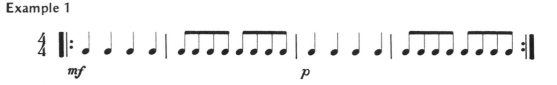

Dynamics are controlled by using beaters of different weights. The percussionist should have two or three different beaters with the triangle.

In order to muffle the triangle, touch the triangle with the last two or three fingers of the hand that is holding the instrument. Practice this technique in the following exercise:

Example 2

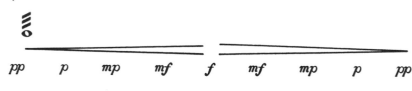

Finally the roll is played by placing the beater in either closed corner and moving it back and forth between the two sides. Dynamics are played by moving the beater further away from the corner. Soft rolls will be played as

close to the corner as possible and loud rolls away from the corner.

Practice the following roll beginning softly, crescendoing, and then growing softer.

Example 3

pp   p   mp   mf   f   mf   mp   p   pp

final thoughts

I sincerely hope that you have enjoyed studying this book and that you will continue enjoying the challenge of percussion. Remember that percussion is the art you make it. You may want to be a symphonic percussionist, a jazz percussionist, invent your own percussion instruments, or perhaps do all three. Whatever you choose, work hard and play with musical creativity. You will find that percussion can add a great deal to your life.

Peter Magadini

Here is a sample adjudication form for solo contest. Under each category comments are made to show you what a judge might consider while you are playing. Since these forms vary slightly, you may want to ask your director to show you an adjudication form from your particular state before you go to contest.

Event No. _____ Order or Time of Appearance _____ Class_____

Name of Soloist_____

School _____District_____ City _____State_____

Instrument_____

Name of Selection _____

	Rating				
	I	II	III	IV	V
	Superior	Very Good	Average	Fair	Poor

TONE (Beauty, Control, Characteristic Timbre, Quality, Volume, Embouchure)

The judge will be listening for the clear, rich tone characteristic of the instrument. He will also be judging how well you control the tone in the different registers and at different dynamic levels. He will make comments on what you need to improve, such as slight changes in your embouchure or the way you hold your instrument.

INTONATION (Melodic Line, Intervals, High and Low Registers)

Intonation is the ability to play in tune. The judge will be listening to your intonation in all registers, and in moving from one note to another especially in large intervals. You should check your part and the accompaniment. If there are any unison notes with the piano, work on getting these in tune.

RHYTHMIC ACCURACY (Accents, Meter, Precision, Interpretation of Rhythmic Figures)

In this category the judge will be listening for rhythmic accuracy. He may make comments about the overall solo or about particular figures within the solo. He will be listening to how precisely and evenly you play eighth notes, sixteenth notes, and triplets and how steady you keep the rhythm throughout the solo.

INTERPRETATION (Phrasing, Expression, Tempo, Dynamics, Style)

Here the judge will be interested in how musically you play. This can be determined by how much expression you use, how well you understand the style of the composition, how wide a range of dynamic levels you can control, and how well you understand the construction of the melodic lines and phrases.

TECHNIQUE (Facility, Articulation, Fingering, Breathing, Attacks, Tonguing)

Although the judge will probably not be able to see specific fingerings you are using, he can tell how much agility and how much control you have by listening to how smoothly and evenly you play. If he hears an area that sounds rough, he may suggest you try to find alternate fingerings that will make the passage easier. He will also be listening as to how accurately you play the marked articulations and how well you can tongue.

SELECTION (Suitability, Musical Value)

The judge will comment on the suitability of the solo, taking into consideration your technical ability, the occasion (contest), and the musical value. If it's too difficult, he may suggest that next year you choose a solo that is easier and that you can perform well. If it is too easy, he may suggest that you choose a solo which is more difficult.

APPEARANCE (Posture, Stage Presence)

Your personal appearance can have a great affect upon the judge's decision. If you and your accompanist are neatly dressed and project a feeling of confidence, he will think you are well-prepared and consider the contest an important event. Be sure your posture is good and your accompanist sits up and is alert.

MEMORIZATION

Some states require that the solo be memorized before a rating will be given. If you have a problem while you are playing, the judge may give you suggestions that will help you memorize more efficiently. For instance, study the solo to find sections that are exactly the same or only slightly different. It may be easier to divide the solo into parts and memorize those before putting the solo together.

ACCOMPANIST (Accuracy, Effectiveness)

This category should not be considered in your rating, but the judge may comment about your accompanist... the difficulty of the accompaniment for the pianist, whether it is apparent that you rehearsed with each other, or the balance between the soloist and the accompanist. He may also mention specific sections of the music which need more practice or techniques which need improvement.